Hide but Seek

Mishti Verma

ZORBA BOOKS

ZORBA BOOKS

Published by Zorba Books, June 2025
Website: www.zorbabooks.com
Email: info@zorbabooks.com
Author Name: Mishti Verma

Title: Hide But Seek

Printbook ISBN: 978-93-5896-192-8
Ebook ISBN: 978-93-5896-544-5

Zorba Books Pvt. Ltd. (opc)
Sushant Arcade,
Next to Courtyard Marriot,
Sushant Lok 1, Gurgaon – 122009, India

Printed in India

For My Family: The First to Listen.

Contents

Preface

I didn't write this book!

This book wasn't written; it was heard. It's an echo of the thousands of women I've had the privilege to connect with, their professional journeys and personal truths whispering to be shared.

It's a reflection of my experiences and the stories I've encountered while working with over 7,000 women professionals, embracing their diverse perspectives across different life stages.

The insights within these pages are drawn from deeper coaching conversations, capturing the nuances of gendered experiences. As you read, you might recognise not just my voice, but an echo of your own heart, perhaps the wisdom of your mother, the resilience of a colleague, or the quiet observations of a neighbour or a woman you pass on the street.

Expressive arts and poetry have been powerful tools in this journey of self-inquiry. Poetry, as the language of the soul, often articulates what words alone cannot.

My connection with the arts began early, at the age of two and a half, and my first performance sparked a lifelong love for the stage. Working with legendary theatre veterans like Tom Alter and Nadira Zaheer Babbar further revealed the magic of theatre.

My training in expressive arts therapy and psychodrama, guided by global experts, deepened my understanding of expressive arts as a medium for profound transformation. It not only impacted my own life but also enriched my learning interventions, fostering strong dialogues and safe spaces for exploring Diversity, Equity, and Inclusion.

This book carries the imprint of gratitude. I want to acknowledge my teachers from various trainings, certifications, and post-graduate diploma programs in expressive arts therapy and psychodrama: Sue Daniel, Jennie Kristel, Magdalene Jeyarathnam, Susan Anand, Saphira Linden, Susan Perrow, Katia Verreault, Dr. Eric Miller, Norma Kay Lord (whom I just started my training with) and Dr. Herb Propper. Though some names mentioned here are no longer with us, their wisdom remains etched in our hearts.

Within these pages, you will also find the powerful, dramatised story of Dr. Preeti Monga, the first visually impaired aerobic trainer and a celebrated voice in DEI. Her story was first shared at our gender sensitisation forum with leading HR institutions like NHRD.

A big thank you to global leadership coaches and expressive arts therapists Colleen Qvist and Jennie Kristel for the beautiful contributions to the book.

For two decades, I've been immersed in the world of learning & development, passionately integrating theatre and the arts into the vital work of gender sensitisation, diversity, and Inclusion.

This experience has built a deep well of expertise in DEIB consulting and leadership coaching. Furthermore, as a Gallup Global Strengths Coach, I have come to believe that focusing on positive psychology and strengths is the foremost way of achieving excellence.

This book offers a powerful intersection of coaching and the liberation offered by expressive arts. There are many resources included to help you navigate life's challenges and gender expectations.

While drawing upon compelling concepts from philosophy, expressive arts, and psychodrama, my priority has been to maintain a wider view and accessible approach, encouraging curiosity and your own deeper dive through the suggested readings and publicly available resources.

If you're ready to embrace who you truly are, beyond what the world wants you to be, to step out of the hidden shadows within and seek your unfiltered truth, then together, let's begin.

Foreword 1

In a world increasingly driven by polarization, masculine anger, aggressive stances and parochialism, comes this book, a gateway into a worldview defined by creative feminine energy, which is both individualistic and collaborative at the same time, a voice that is equally a chorus, reminiscent of the Greek tragedies, as well as a solo refrain of a diva in all her operatic glory.

Mishti shares with us powerful gender themes that are distinct and yet universal, based on an extensive body of work, representing thousands of women she has coached and mentored. In small ways and big, the trials and tribulations we have faced and continue to face in a world which still thinks of fifty percent of its population as the minority remain exactly and sadly the same.

When all of us who are committed to making this world an equal and a fair one argue the case for DEI, we increasingly face push back from those who would prefer the status quo to be maintained or worse, would prefer that the gains we have made in the last few decades get wiped out by a change in law or by redeploying and reducing resources that have been working hard to close the gender gap.

In such a world, how do we fight back? What shall we teach our sisters and our daughters?

And that is where I invite you to join in a movement where you continue to make your voice heard, your opinions loud and clear, as you stand tall and straight in your posture of a warrior queen. Much as the world tries to drown out your individuality and pushes you to become a cipher, you must work hard to regain your agency, to drown out not only the external negating forces but equally the voice in your heart and mind that is telling you that you are not good enough. The years of socialization that have told you to adapt and accommodate, to put your needs and desires last, to not rock the boat, need to be wiped out from your psyche.

However, to make your voice heard and your opinions matter, you require to strengthen your muscle of choice, one small decision made one step at a time. Equally you require the tools to express these choices and these opinions freely and fully.

Hide but Seek is not only a powerful weapon that will help you become stronger, it is a guide for personal transformation, providing practical techniques and connecting you to the strength and wisdom of women across history and cultures.

– Apurva Purohit

Co-Founder Aazol | Independent Director | Best-selling Author – Lady, You're the Boss | Lady, You're not a Man

Ex-President – Jagran Prakashan Ltd | Ex CEO – Radio City, recognized as one of the 'Most Powerful Women in Business' by India Today Group and Fortune India.

Foreword 2

"This book is a unique and powerful resource, drawing on the author's rich experience in coaching women through life's complexities. By interweaving expressive arts with practical guidance, the author provides a pathway for women to unlock their innate feminine power. Through anecdotes and insightful reflections, the book addresses critical issues around gender roles, male dominance, and the urgent need for gender sensitivity, offering a compelling vision for personal and collective healing. The author, Mishti Verma, is a very hard working and talented student of mine, who worked with me from 1994 to 1997.

Recently, I came to know about her work for women, specifically highlighting the challenges of working women.

I am very happy that she is using theatre as a medium of communication to put her thoughts across.

I congratulate her for the new upcoming book and wish her all the good luck and success for the same and for her life too."

– Nadira Zaheer Babbar

Renowned theatre personality, acclaimed director, writer, and actress in Theatre and Cinema, recipient of Sangeet Natak Akademi Award. Founder of a Mumbai-based theatre group, Ekjute.

CHAPTER 1

Inner Katha – The Hidden Story Within

I was inspired to launch my experiential learning company in March 2008.

I use the word inspired because any process of creation comes from 'a muse' or inspiration.

So, who was this muse in my life? Well, nothing external, but a little voice inside —a soul whisper — that pushed me to listen not just to my own voice, but also to the quiet knocks of many other lives.

The first campaign we launched for Inner Katha was for women managers—a rallying cry for self-expression over suppression. Our research interviews with over two hundred women at different managerial levels across India revealed that women often measured their self-worth based on their social roles. The question they often asked themselves was – Am I a 'good mother,' 'good daughter,' 'good manager?'

The key word being—'good,' perhaps stemming from cultural conditioning that focuses on 'shoulds' and being a "good girl."

The voices of the world had already drawn the 'Lakshman Rekha' and social barriers of – WHAT ONE SHOULD DO and how important it was to continue the generational burden of being a "good girl."

No wonder the voice of doubt continues to ring a bell even as we grow up, and one questions, 'Am I the good daughter, the good wife, the good professional?' and not if one is great enough but wondering, 'Am I good enough?'

Sometimes, this inner feeling can also lead to the "IMPOSTOR syndrome." Even if you have achieved great success, you may still question, 'Do I really deserve this? Am I really good enough?' You are capable, you are skilled, and you deserve every success you've achieved. Yet, that inner critic might still pipe up, making you question your worthiness. This is the hallmark of impostor syndrome, a common experience where feelings of inadequacy persist despite external validation.

Despite the inner arguments and turmoil, quite often, 'the good girl' doesn't raise an argument. If she voices her opinion strongly, she may be seen as aggressive and ill-mannered.

Recognising the suppression this causes, we intentionally focused on creating a safe space within our workshops for women to feel heard and acknowledged.

Perhaps that is why our first leadership program brought in the rain, not just because it was the onset of the monsoon but because we facilitated a program where women managers felt safe enough to shed their corporate identities and express fully suppressed emotions. They shared laughter and tears. Yes, it rained that day, and I saw the power of tears.

It reminded me of the women's circle rituals in different cultures. The Rudaali ritual in Rajasthan is a unique tradition with cultural significance. It involves women from specific lower castes who are hired as professional mourners to publicly express grief at the death of a higher-caste male.

The Rudaali tradition arose in a society where upper-caste women were often secluded and restricted from publicly displaying strong emotions, especially grief. This created a need for an outlet for mourning, which was filled by the Rudaalis. Rudaalis typically wear black, a colour of mourning in many cultures. Their performance involves loud weeping, chest-beating, and sometimes even singing mournful songs.

The cultural metaphor of Rudaalis reminded me how we are conditioned to suppress our feelings and sometimes need a support circle or a ritual for these feelings to be projected or expressed.

In conducting over 1000 workshops on gender diversity, a powerful pattern has emerged.

Engaging with sensitive gender themes through experiential learning and applied theatre has broken down barriers, cultivating dialogues and emotions that transcend gender, and ultimately crafting unifying experiences of the heart.

Somewhere at the corner of the room, I, too, have had tears streaming down; perhaps we all have a story to tell, and there are stories trapped within.

The poem in this essay gives voice to the story and feelings of many women I've worked with—their Inner Katha!

Ran

As fast as I could
I ran
Didn't know where to go
Nameless streets, no sign, no man
As fast as I could
I ran
Waiting for a turn
Waiting for a voice
No clues, no noise
Silence of fate
Endless wait
As fast as I could
I ran
I ran
As fast as I could
From where I stood
A silent image

Bleeding hearts, dark bondage
The first or last sign
I don't want to see
Another image of me

As fast as I could
I ran
Sometimes, fate does speak
I play a game with myself
It is called 'Hide and Seek'
As fast as I could
I ran

Far far away
I want to stay. Can it be another world?
Or just another day?

Where you can love and smile
Not just for a while
Where you are free from fears
Not bound by tears
Where words are yours to express
Not for others to judge or oppress

Where you can be
All that you want to be
Where, on a mountain top
You can shout and scream
This dream is mine to dream!

– Mishti Verma

CHAPTER 2

The Guide – Seeking Emotions!

In his poem "The Guesthouse," the famous poet Rumi talks about emotions as a guide.

Sharing this powerful poem:

The Guesthouse

This being human is a guest house. Every morning a new arrival.
A joy, a depression, a meanness, some momentary awareness comes
as an unexpected visitor. Welcome and entertain them all!
Even if they're a crowd of sorrows, who violently sweep your house
empty of its furniture, still, treat each guest honourably.
He may be clearing you out for some new delight.
The dark thought, the shame, the malice, meet them at the door
laughing, and invite them in.

Be grateful for whoever comes, because each has been sent as a guide from beyond.

– Rumi

Each new dawn brings with it a fresh wave of emotion. We might rise with a sense of buoyant happiness, eager to embrace what lies ahead. Or we could find ourselves wrestling with grumpiness, anger, or the weight of sadness.

These emotions, however, are like guests at the door of our inner world. They arrive with a gentle prompting, and if we allow them entry, we might discover the underlying message they hold. Much like the morning newspaper unveils the day's events, our emotions offer insights into the deeper currents of our lives, revealing far more than just the mere headlines.

Breaking news, emotional suppression is real!

I never realised when it started, but I became adept at suppressing my feelings. Actually, I didn't even realise what I was feeling on many occasions. For instance, if someone behaved in a nasty way, my first response would always be one of calm disposition. Much later, I would realise that there was a lot of anger brewing within.

In the coaching world, we explore limiting beliefs that lead to limiting behaviours, and these were some beliefs that led to suppression.

A limiting belief holding me back would be that showing anger was a sign of disrespect!

Another limiting belief was that I was a "cultured" girl, so I should keep my anger in check!

When anger within us is bottled up for long, it either results in sudden outbursts or, at times, a psychological defense mechanism known as 'displacement' of anger. It means that you are angry at one person, but you direct your anger at someone else or something else other than the person you are actually angry with. For example, if you are angry at your boss or manager, but because of the power dynamics, you may choose to keep quiet and then later redirect that anger towards your subordinate, spouse, or children.

In my case, I just swallowed all the anger like a pill, and because of this constant suppression, I developed many health issues for a long period of time.

Anger, like other emotions, is a messenger; it tells you what is beneath the surface and what really needs to be addressed.

The root of my anger was not standing up for myself and not speaking my truth in crucial moments. Not communicating my needs, not drawing boundaries. Not believing that I was truly worthy of love, and that I had the right to assert my needs, be it in a difficult relationship or in a difficult job.

I chose to stay quiet, even when I was at the receiving end of multiple microaggression scenarios.

I had somehow mastered the art of emotional suppression, so much so that there were times I could not even connect with my own body or its sensations and signals.

What truly helped me to cope with emotional suppression was my training in psychodrama and expressive arts therapy. I remember key moments of my psychodrama training, where my anger was fully concretised.

During this group therapy session, my anger was personified through the metaphor of the 'Kali Dance' and I danced in complete glory, giving full expression to my internal rage.

My psychodrama mentor set up the stage for me beautifully, with music and different colours of drapes signifying other aspects of my story.

For me, while embodying the role of Kali Ma, the most significant aspect was my need for the tongue to be fully expressed outward, as in her representation, and to dance fiercely. If I consider these metaphors—"Tongue" and "Dance"—and decode them from my perspective, "Tongue" represents the expression of emotions or voices. "Goddess Kali" symbolizes an empowered, fearless feminine, and "Dance" expresses my very being.

What were these metaphors illustrating? What information was the anger conveying?

To put this in a simple sentence, it was: "I need to be fearless and be an empowered feminine who can speak her truth with courage without withholding expression and express her inner talents freely."

The anger was my guide, and so were the various "NAVRASAS" emotions, like the rain of tears mentioned in the previous essay.

My connection with the goddess has not just begun through expressive arts therapy, but somewhere mystical paths have been opening up, and I have started taking small steps on these roads less travelled by way of bigger leaps of faith...

Connect with Your Feelings: Expressive Arts Therapy Practices

- **Expanding Your Emotional Language:** To better understand and connect with your inner world, make an effort to learn and name your emotions. Building a robust emotional vocabulary can help you engage with your feelings more consistently and move beyond suppression.
- **Colouring Your Inner State: The Emotions Wheel**
    - You will need: Colour pencils.
    - Using an emotions wheel as your guide, identify the emotion you are currently feeling. Choose a colour that speaks to that emotion and colour in the relevant area of the wheel.

Emotions Wheel

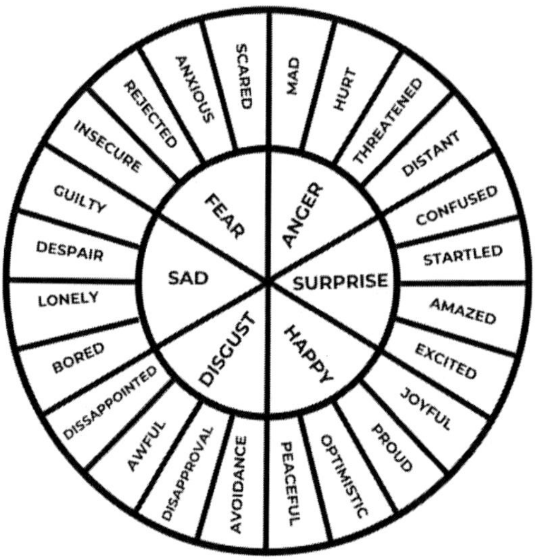

Emotional Awareness Journaling Prompts

Reflect on your emotions today using the following:

- **Emotion Identification: "I am currently feeling [label the emotion]."**
- **Intensity Check-in: On a scale of 1 (mild) to 10 (intense), this emotion feels like a ___. (Consider using colour variations to visually represent this intensity in your journal.)**
- **The Emotion's Message: If this emotion were a guide, what is it trying to tell me?**

Connecting with Your Emotion Through Your Body:

- Your Gesture: Allow your body to express your current feeling through a simple gesture. What movement feels most authentic right now? What message or meaning does this gesture hold for you?
- The Emotion's Dance: Imagine your emotion as a form of movement. What would that movement look like? To deepen this exploration, choose a drape that embodies the colour you feel aligns with this emotion. Let the emotion guide your movement as you hold and move with the drape. Notice any shifts or insights that arise within your body.

Reflecting and Integrating Your Experience:

- Sharing Your Journey (Optional): You might find it helpful to share your experience with a supportive friend or an "emotion buddy" – someone you trust to talk about your feelings openly.
- Journaling for Deeper Understanding: Take some time to reflect on your embodiment experience through journaling. Consider these questions:

- What came up for you during the Embodiment Activity? What thoughts emerged?
- What feelings were present?
- What sensations did you notice in your body? What observations did you make about your physical experience?

CHAPTER 3

The Hidden Boundaries

"I was not making a rangoli, yes I make rangolis of different colours, but here I was not making a rangoli, I was painting my boundaries, drawing the line with the bold colour of red, the colour of the divine feminine, and if you cross these lines, it becomes the colour of feminine rage!"

The tale of the Lakshman Rekha is a prominent story associated with the Hindu epic Ramayana.

The narrative unfolds during Rama, Sita, and Lakshmana's exile in the forest. A captivating golden deer appears, enchanting Sita. Rama pursues the deer, entrusting Sita's protection to Lakshmana.

While Rama is absent, the dying Maricha imitates Rama's voice, calling for help. Hearing this, a worried Sita implores Lakshmana to assist Rama.

Before departing, Lakshmana draws a protective line (the Lakshman Rekha) around their dwelling with his arrow, assuring Sita of her safety within its confines.

Once Lakshmana leaves, Ravana, disguised as a mendicant, approaches Sita seeking alms. Unaware of his true nature, Sita crosses the Lakshman Rekha to offer him food, immediately nullifying the magical protection. Ravana then abducts her.

Symbolically, the Lakshman Rekha represents the vital importance of respecting boundaries, both physical and metaphorical.

What if Sita, empowered by her wisdom and agency, chose to define her own boundaries? What would *her* Lakshman Rekha look like? It wouldn't be a line drawn in the dust, but a complex, multifaceted understanding of her own needs and values.

Sita's "Rekha" might be a circle of respect, not dictated by social norms or disguised sages, but earned through genuine kindness and integrity. It would be a boundary that allowed her to choose who deserved her reverence, regardless of their status or appearance. It would be a shield against unwanted advances, not just physical, but also emotional and manipulative. Her Rekha might be a quiet strength, a refusal to be silenced or diminished.

And if that boundary was to be breached? Then, perhaps, the "Feminine Rage" would rise. Not a blind, uncontrolled fury, but a righteous anger born of violated trust and disregarded autonomy. It would be the voice of a woman who knows her worth and refuses to be a victim.

The mythological re-telling of Draupadi's inner wounding in Mahabharata is a strong example of the embodiment of "Feminine Rage."

Draupadi's rage is a complex and multifaceted aspect of her character in the Mahabharata. It stems from the numerous injustices and humiliations she faces throughout her life, and it plays a significant role in shaping the narrative of the epic.

Her rage becomes a catalyst for the Kurukshetra war. Her vow not to tie her hair until it is washed with the blood of Dushasana, the man who disrobed her, serves as a powerful motivation for the Pandavas to seek revenge. Speaking up and taking a strong stand, a symbol of feminine power and resistance against patriarchal oppression, it challenges the traditional notions of female submissiveness and passivity.

Beyond the well-worn narratives of mythology and history, the boundaries of gender emerge as both fragile and formidable. They are the lines, often unspoken, that we trace around ourselves, defining who we are in relation to the world. And, perhaps most importantly, they are the bedrock of our sense of safety. Without these boundaries, we are adrift, vulnerable. We need them to feel secure in our identities, to know our place, and to safeguard our physical and emotional well-being.

Boundaries are not always visible, though; they are not the concrete 'gates' or boundary walls for safety. Some boundaries are hidden. What are these hidden boundaries?

For a woman, it is a combination of physical, mental, emotional, moral, and cultural boundaries.

We're taught about physical boundaries, the difference between a "good touch" and a "bad touch," but emotional boundaries are often invisible, hidden beneath the surface. These unseen lines define our inner needs, our self-expression, and our emotional safety – the spaces where we can be ourselves without fear of judgment, punishment, or shame.

These boundaries are violated through constant suppression. They're breached when we're denied the chance to voice our feelings, to even understand what makes us comfortable or uncomfortable, what our inner needs truly are. They are violated when we're robbed of the freedom to choose – whether it's our career or our life partner. This theft of agency often happens under the guise of patriarchal notions of morality, family pride, or 'protection,' or through the unwanted influence of relatives.

When the self's expression is stifled, caged by the rigid bars of family expectations or societal decrees, the invisible lines of personal boundaries harden into walls. As the walls ascend, so too does the internal chaos. The inevitable consequence is a choice between two paths: a defiant eruption, a rebellion against the constricting forces, or a slow, simmering rage, a fire smouldering in the depths of the soul, waiting for its moment to ignite.

I was working with a client who had gone through strong episodes of beating and physical abuse in her childhood. Through constant criticism and judgment, she started suppressing her inner needs and voice. She had developed the belief that if she spoke up, she would be judged or criticised.

It stemmed from the belief that women should remain silent and adjust. This, in turn, led to low self-esteem, and slowly she started building strong walls around herself. That led to recurrent challenges in building long-term relationships.

To break the walls, we needed to first work on understanding and honouring 'the hidden boundaries' and most definitely understanding and honouring the deep-seated anger.

A good way to understand boundaries is by understanding our needs, choices and personal space. We have often heard the line "I need my space!" Personal space is the invisible bubble each of us maintains, and it's important for women to understand this concept in different life spaces, including its importance at the workplace.

The size of this bubble isn't fixed and varies depending on:

- Cultural Norms: Expectations about personal space differ across cultures. Awareness of this can help prevent misunderstandings in diverse personal and work environments.
- Personal Preferences: Everyone has their own comfort level. It's crucial to recognise and respect your own needs and be considerate of others.
- Relationship Dynamics: The closer the relationship, the smaller the bubble. You'll naturally have different space needs with close colleagues versus new acquaintances.

'Proxemics' is a powerful concept that helps us understand the nuances of personal space.

Edward T. Hall, a prominent proxemics researcher, identified four zones of interpersonal distance:

- Intimate Distance (0-18 inches): Typically reserved for close relationships; generally inappropriate for the workplace.
- Personal Distance (1.5-4 feet): Suitable for casual conversations with colleagues.

- Social Distance (4-12 feet): The standard for most professional interactions.
- Public Distance (12 feet and beyond): Used for formal presentations and public speaking.

Territoriality and Crowding in the Workplace

Two additional concepts are key for women to navigate in the workplace:

- Territoriality: This is the need to claim and defend your space, whether it's your desk, office, or shared resources. Understanding this can help women advocate for their needs.
- Crowding: This is the feeling of discomfort from a perceived lack of space, even if the area is physically large. Being mindful of this can contribute to a more comfortable work environment.

Embracing spaces and learning about boundaries, the soul whispers to the world-*"Blur the lines but don't blur the vision, the vision of a future, where birds are not caged, but can fly beyond the horizon and sing their own song."*

Expressive Arts Activity: Exploring Your Personal Space

This activity will help you visualise and reflect on your personal space.

1. Draw a circle. Inside the circle, create a collage of pictures that represent your personal space. Choose pictures of relationships, cultural and moral drivers, and personal preferences.

2. Journal Prompts After the Activity:
   a) Look at the collage and reflect: What would you like to see more of in your personal space? How big or small is your personal space circle?
   b) What would you like to see less of in your personal space circle?
   c) Complete the sentence: My hidden boundaries are...
   d) I can honour my hidden boundaries by taking these small steps or actions: (Write down three actions.)

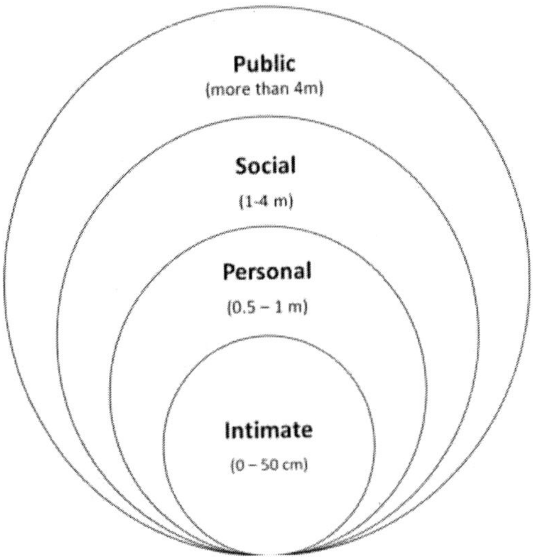

Activity: Mapping Your Proxemic Zones

Materials: Crayons or coloured pencils

1. **Visual Representation:** Using the provided diagram, colour each proxemic zone (Intimate, Personal, Social, and Public) with a distinct colour.
2. **Emotional Connection:** For each coloured zone, write down three feelings that arise as you consider that space.

3. **Personal Reflection:** Journal your reflections on these proxemic zones. Consider the following questions:
    - How do these zones affect your interactions and relationships?
    - How do you currently navigate these zones in your daily life?
    - Are there any zones where you feel particularly comfortable or uncomfortable?
    - What insights have you gained about your personal space and boundaries?

CHAPTER 4

Seeking the Courage to Say NO!

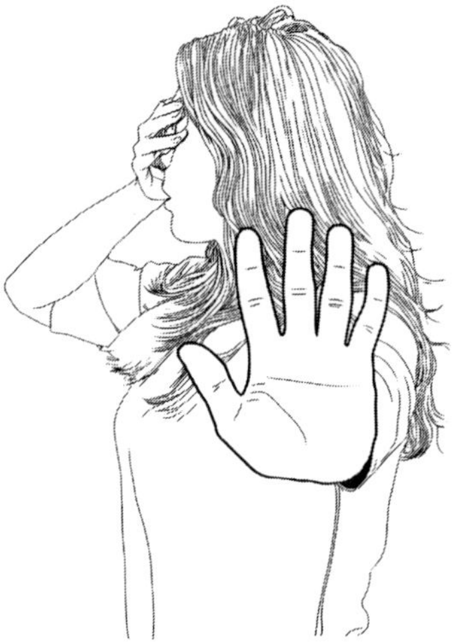

"'No' was a seed, planted deep within. But then, when the moment of the test arrived –

I heard myself say the word 'Yes' and the sound of betrayal. It wasn't a word, but a hollow echo, a crack in the carefully constructed walls of my resolve, letting in the chill of doubt.

It was like mirthless laughter, a helpless, hollow jest. It was my own reflection in the mirror, mocking my unrest."

I lead a workshop for women on the 'Power to say No' – based on multiple organisation and gender narratives. The discoveries often make me wonder – why do we need 'power' to say NO?

Why does saying 'no' feel so unnatural? The stark reality, revealed in countless candid conversations during my workshops, is that many women harbour a profound fear. They struggle to muster the courage to simply say 'no.' This fear manifests in various situations: declining projects despite overwork, disagreeing in meetings, refusing unnecessary domestic burdens, rejecting unwanted food or clothing, exiting unfulfilling relationships, and, fundamentally, pushing back against the 'extras' when their plates are already overflowing.

When I ask participants, 'What will happen if you say no?' A deep insecurity often surfaces. The worry of judgment is palpable, accompanied by a persistent question: 'Am I good enough?' 'Will I fail to meet expectations in my career or family?'

This struggle is captured in a line from my play on gender sensitisation – *Zubaan*: *"Agar mein chaar logon ka khayal bhi na rakh payee, khush na rakh saki toh mera vajood kya hai?"*

This may sound regressive, but it comes up in sharing circles.

"If I cannot take care of my loved ones or make even four people happy, then what is the worth of my existence?"

As a child, I lived true to my name – 'Mishti,' and always behaved like a sweet, soft-spoken girl. I believed that my sweetness should not cause any bitterness. Growing up, 'no' was a word seldom spoken. Raised to prioritise politeness, I feared causing hurt, leading to a pattern of self-sacrifice and blurred personal boundaries. It took a series of painful experiences in life to understand that embracing my own 'yes' required saying 'no' to many other things. I recall a moment from a past relationship. He asked me to fetch his shoes. Though I lacked the courage to say 'no,' an inner voice strongly resisted. Caught in that conflict, I simply walked away silently, never speaking to him again. I realised that, despite potential hurt, it was essential for my own well-being and protection to say 'NO.' And say yes, only when you truly feel like saying yes. This realisation ignited a journey of building inner strength and assertiveness. Through conscious practice and a spiritual connection with the Goddess & Shakti, I cultivated the courage to stand my ground. My self-perception shifted, evolving from a sweet little girl to a determined leader. I haven't abandoned that sweet inner child; rather, I've gently guided her, releasing limiting beliefs and leading her towards a path of empowerment.

Learning to say 'no' empowers you to prioritise effectively, establish healthy boundaries, achieve work-life balance, and make space for what truly matters. Here are practical exercises to cultivate this skill:

1. **Practice in Low-Stakes Situations:** Build courage by saying 'no' to requests or situations where the consequences are minimal.
2. **Affirm Your Worth:** Strengthen self-belief by repeating daily affirmations in the mirror for 21 days: I believe in myself. I am worthy of respect. I am worthy of love.
3. **Reflective Journaling:** Explore your resistance to 'no' with these prompts: What prevents me from saying 'no?' What support do I need? What limiting beliefs hold me back?
4. **Visualise Empowerment:** Create a collage of images that represent an empowered self, one capable of confidently saying 'no' and asserting personal rights. Write down a few words that describe the collage.

CHAPTER 5

The Veil – Hiding Identity

The Veil

She would cover her head with a veil,
A kind smile and eyes kohled with shyness.
One day the veil flew away and got trapped in the world maze.
Unveiled and frightened of a judging gaze, she began to find her way out.
She met some who said, "start a revolution," Or "wait for some kind of evolution."
The maze and mirrored reflections,
Some dark shadows, some dazzling light.

Finding her way, she met some who advised her to play a game of chess.
They said, "It's a way out of the maze."
Amazed, she chose love over a game of power.
Mirrored reflections,
Finding her in some and some in others,
Reflecting life in different hues.
Unveiled with flowing dark hair, a kind smile and eyes shining with fiery coal,
Finding her way, the maze transformed into a prism,
Reflecting light and the promise of a rainbow.

– Mishti Verma

The "ghonghaat," or veil, in Indian Hindu culture traditionally served to shield a woman from the male gaze and symbolise "maryada," an adherence to societal norms. While the physical veil has largely disappeared in modern urban settings, the concept of "covering" persists. For example, a female manager recounted having to conceal family photos during performance reviews, fearing her manager would perceive her as prioritising home over career advancement, thus hindering her promotion, which required extensive travel.

The need to project strength in professional settings often leads women to downplay their feminine qualities and hide behind the masculine. It's a phenomenon reminiscent of old advertisements that equated smoking with masculine power. In a women's leadership program for a well-known media company, I witnessed women recognising how they unconsciously adopted "masculine" behaviours—toughness, emotional detachment—to be seen as leaders. They also pointed out the importance of cigarette breaks for networking, with some admitting to starting smoking themselves.

After a leadership retreat, one woman poignantly realised she had lost touch with her inner femininity, having spent years in a provider role, and expressed a desire to reclaim that balance.

This was not the first time; many of my coaching clients have shared similar experiences.

During an art therapy session, a client's drawing revealed a profound need for control. Her rigid, heavily bordered lines trapped her colours, preventing expression beyond structured patterns. This mirrored her life: always in charge, the provider, the responsible one. Yet, as she began to release her grip, to reclaim her feminine essence through practices of flow, rest, and receiving, a remarkable shift occurred. Her drawings softened. The harsh lines gave way to fluid strokes, and she embraced vibrant hues of pink and watercolour washes, embodying a newfound sense of ease. This transformation illustrated a universal truth: within each of us, regardless of gender, resides both masculine and feminine energies. The masculine provides direction, focus, logic, strength, and protection, while the feminine is associated with creation, intuition, emotion, flow, and connection.

Sometimes, history reveals its most compelling stories in whispers. The tales of women who, with extraordinary bravery, disguised themselves as men to fight are among them. Loreta Janeta Velazquez, an American woman, masqueraded as a male soldier. Harry T. Buford, fought in the Civil War, leaving behind her own account in the book, "The Woman in Battle."

She also worked as a spy in male and female disguises, reporting to the U.S. secret services.

There's also another kind of warrior woman, one who doesn't need to borrow another's identity.

Picture this: Delhi, a city simmering with unrest. Amidst the chaos of a violent protest against the Nirankari Samagam near India Gate, a figure of quiet authority stood firm. A Twenty-nine-year-old Deputy Commissioner of Police, standing tall as a woman warrior. While demonstrators threatened to breach the police cordon, Kiran Bedi, a woman of resolute spirit, became the unexpected anchor. With a commanding presence, she rallied the wavering ranks of the police force, her unwavering resolve a tangible force that ultimately quelled the surging mob.

Imagine the scene painted by Subhadra Kumari Chauhan's iconic poem on the Queen of Jhansi. Picture the valiant Rani, perhaps even with her child, facing the might of the British.

The poem, with its powerful lines like "Chamak uthi san sattavan mein, yeh talwar purani thi," immortalises her courage, a courage recounted by the Bundela Harbolas: "Khoob ladi mardani woh to Jhansi wali Rani thi." This wasn't a display of borrowed masculinity, but a fierce feminine strength.

These women fought as women, igniting a warrior spirit embodied by a woman in her full capacity, her power undeniable even in the face of vulnerability.

As I listen to these stories, a familiar tug resonates within my heart. I recognise a past where I, too, inadvertently sidelined my feminine essence, perhaps even judging it as soft or weak.

When life hit me hard, I instinctively donned the armour of the masculine. My journey towards self-discovery has led me to a deep realisation: I must honour the feminine within. I owe her an apology for neglecting her, for the judgments I held, for not heeding her quiet wisdom – a silencing that mirrors societal norms. Now, I choose to let her lead, a warrior of light, while my inner masculine gently offers support. This, I believe, is the shift our society needs: when women choose to lead, may others choose to be their allies. It's time to drop the metaphorical 'ghoonghat,' to shed our filters and present ourselves authentically, applauding our greatest talents and strengths.

Engage in a creative exercise to explore your feminine energy.

Mandala Creation:

Begin by drawing a mandala, a sacred circle that will hold your exploration. Within this space, use the expressive power of colours and paints to give form to your inner feminine. Let the colour red be a key element, alongside any other hues that intuitively arise. Enhance your creation with textures and sparkle – perhaps glitter, feathers, or any material that feels meaningful to you.

<u>Journaling for Insight:</u>

Consider the following questions in your journal:

- ❖ **What are the visual characteristics of my inner feminine?**
- ❖ **What messages or guidance is my inner feminine offering?**
- ❖ **What does she require to feel seen, heard, and secure?**
- ❖ **What actions can I take to honour and acknowledge her?**

CHAPTER 6

Seeking Identity

The hesitant lift of the 'ghoonghat' is a gesture imbued with duality. Sometimes, it mirrors the shy surrender of a bride stepping into a new life. Other times, and perhaps more profoundly, it marks a metaphorical unveiling of the true self, a shedding of layers long held. In this delicate unravelling of identity, the individual often carries the heavy weight of shame and the sharp, unsettling fear of a merciless judgmental gaze.

This vulnerability is a legacy for women, their journey of self-expression historically burdened by societal shaming. The witch hunts stand as a brutal, indelible mark on history, a time when women who embraced their unique "magic" and sacred understanding were not celebrated but hunted down for their very essence.

Despite the advancements of modern times, where women have undeniably proven their strength and earned global acclaim, the debris of internalised shame for simply being themselves still reaches into the present. We see its reflection in the intimate landscapes of personal choice – the way a woman chooses to dress, the exploration of her sexuality, and the entirety of her individual way of being.

To seek the true self, one must consciously choose to let go of internalised shame and recognise when the shame stems from within and when it has been projected by society.

This choice may stir up an inner chaos that gives birth to the fullness of identity. The acclaimed, late 19th-century German philosopher Friedrich Nietzsche beautifully encapsulated this essence with the powerful quote: "You must have chaos within you to give birth to a dancing star!"

This influential thinker, a scholar of classical languages and a sharp critic of the prevailing culture of his time, fundamentally challenged the comfortable notion of a fixed and stable "self."

For Nietzsche, the self is not a static idol carved in stone but a dynamic river, its waters constantly flowing with drives, interpretations, and the ever-shifting currents of experience.

True identity, he argued, is a vibrant tapestry to be woven, thread by painstaking thread. It is an active creation, a continuous journey of "becoming what one is." It is a relentless process of self-overcoming and the deliberate, artful shaping of one's character, much like a potter moulds clay upon the wheel. The driving force behind this creation is the "will to power" – not a crude lust for dominance, but a fundamental, life-affirming yearning for growth, self-mastery, and a profound embrace of existence in all its complexity.

He was a vocal critic of what he termed "herd morality," the often-unexamined, traditional, social and religious values that prioritise conformity and subtly, or not so subtly, suppress the bold expression of individual uniqueness. Nietzsche's ideal, the "sovereign individual," possesses the courage to break free from the familiar shackles of external constraints and societal expectations, taking full ownership of their own values.

A dancing star charting its own course beyond the constellations and the vast expanse of the night sky.

The pioneering psychiatrist and founder of psychodrama, Dr. J.L. Moreno, offered a profound understanding of the self, viewing it not as a fixed entity but as an expansive force revealed through the multiple roles we inhabit. He articulated this beautifully: "Roles do not emerge from the self, but a sense of self emerges from the roles we play." To truly understand ourselves, it becomes insightful to explore the different roles and facets that reside within us. Each role carries its own unique narrative, and by acknowledging and understanding these internal players, we gain clarity about our deepest needs, aspirations, and the connections we yearn for.

Growing up, the archetype of the compassionate mother lived vividly within me. Those closest to me affectionately called me 'Mother India,' a testament to the nurturing care that seemed to flow endlessly from me. Yet, as life unfolded, the voice of this maternal role grew quiet. Professional ambitions took center stage, and the challenges of navigating life, including the complexities of a broken marriage, absorbed my focus. The traditional pathways to motherhood remained closed off.

Then, a few years ago, a stirring began within. A deep sensation arose, as if my very womb was yearning, longing to bring forth life. My breasts felt a phantom fullness, an ache to nourish and cradle a baby. A silent lullaby echoed in the quiet corners of my heart, a melody with no one to sing it to.

It took months of gentle self-acceptance to truly acknowledge this resurfacing role, to understand that I first needed to shed old, limiting narratives about my identity. I was not solely defined by my professional achievements, my role as a daughter, or my resilience as a warrior. The mother archetype resided within, a vital part of who I was. Confusion arose, tangled with the realities of age, perimenopause, and life as a single woman. How could I possibly do justice to this profound yearning within the practical constraints of my life? My mind felt like a cage built of practicalities.

To break free, I realised I needed to let go of an outdated version of myself, to dismantle the rigid gender narratives that often confine us to narrow choices. At my core, at a fundamental level of being, I was 'Ma,' even if that motherhood would not express itself in traditional ways. I found myself drawn to an orphanage, showering love and attention on those who needed the shelter of nurturing. I consciously channelled my inner mother in sessions and workshops, embodying unconditional love and acceptance, offering a healing light to the wounds held in trapped spaces.

Perhaps the 'how' of embracing motherhood in conventional terms remains unwritten in my life story, but I now understand the essential first steps in embodying any role or part within us: a gentle, kind embrace; understanding the 'why;' a willingness to overcome internal resistance, and a deep listening to the inner voice.

The journey of embracing our identity is a continuous process of acceptance and recognition, a constant attunement to the ever-evolving self and the diverse songs of the soul. It requires us to acknowledge all the parts within, even those that feel uncomfortable or reside in the shadows, for it is in this wholeness that true understanding and integration lie.

What do these shadow selves look like? In my case, perhaps like a leader with a ruthless streak, wanting to 'go for the kill,' something that can surface in my entrepreneurial drive to lead, acquire, and strategise. Though a fuller exploration warrants a separate discussion, I've come to understand the importance of aligning even these traits with a higher purpose and light.

Death of a Different Order!

She refused she had died,
Burning in flames,
Giving birth to an inner fire.
Yes, there was death, but the death of a different order.
She had bled, but the blood was not of an unhealed wound,
But the blood of a beautiful menstrual river, the blood of a warrior who had won an inner battle,
Triumphing over her own shadows,
Breaking all shackles.
And as the sun set, with the last drop of blood, tears and fears,
She had died, leaving an identity that no longer served her,
Shedding all that she was not.
She had died as warrior claiming the light,
And now she danced in bliss, in love of an eternal kind,
With the unconquerable lightness of being.

– Mishti Verma

Activity: Exploration for self-discovery

This activity invites you to explore different facets of yourself through the creation of a character.

1. **Character Selection:** If you were to play a role in a movie, theatre act, or story, what character would you choose?
2. **Character Description:**
    - What would this character look like?
    - What personality traits would they possess?

- What core values would guide their actions?
- What goals would they strive to achieve?

3. **Character's Voice:**
    - If this character had a popular dialogue or catchphrase, what would it be?
    - Write a monologue or speech for this character. What central message would the character convey?
4. **Reflection:** What message does this character have for you?

CHAPTER 7

Hiding Behind the Superhero

In modern-day homes, the pervasive glow of iPad screens often eclipses the natural light filtering through the windows, keeping children absorbed in digital worlds, seemingly unaware of the vibrant colours of nature just beyond their reach. Though the fantastical realms of superhero games and AI may captivate a child's imagination, the real heroes they instinctively seek are much closer to home.

These steadfast figures, in our homes, skilfully navigate the relentless pressures of professional obligations alongside the intricate demands of home and family. They are the providers and the protectors, often shielding their children from life's harsh realities, even at the cost of their own needs. While the ideal of shared responsibility between partners, regardless of gender, is gaining traction, the weight of this "double burden" still disproportionately falls upon women in many parts of the country. The 2011 Nielsen Survey found that a huge number of Indian women, over 87%, felt stressed regularly. This was a lot more than the stress reported by women in other countries.

It was this phenomenon that prompted the 2015 launch of "Bahu versus Bottomline," our theatre-based program designed to explore the complexities of this double burden syndrome. While societal norms are evolving, with partners increasingly sharing household chores, the survey data underscored a persistent truth: women in India often shoulder the lion's share of domestic responsibilities.

A key theme that resonated deeply through our program was the pervasive presence of 'guilt.' More often than not, women carry a profound sense of guilt, a hidden nest of anxiety coexisting with the nurturing nest of a home they have so carefully built.

In one poignant scene from "Bahu versus Bottomline," we offered a glimpse into this lived experience: a woman torn between the urgent demands of project deadlines and the need to rush home and comfort her crying child. This seemingly simple depiction invariably triggered a powerful emotional response in our audiences, with many women experiencing a kindred resonance and an upheaval of deeply held feelings.

The relentless pressures these "sheroes" face often take a significant toll on their well-being, paving a direct path to burnout. Recognising the insidious signs of this exhaustion becomes paramount.

It is essential for women to prioritise – to deliberately declutter their lives – not just their physical spaces, but also their mental and emotional landscapes. Focusing on their own well-being and consciously letting go of commitments and concerns that no longer serve them are crucial acts of self-care.

In my mentoring work with women executives, I often use a simple yet resonant analogy.

I encourage them to consider their closets. Is there a dress, a garment, lingering within, held onto with the hopeful notion that one day they will "fit in?" This mirrors the way they often try to conform to a multitude of social roles and expectations, stretching themselves thin in the process. I invite them to engage in a deeper reflection, to identify what they can declutter not only from their wardrobes but also from their inboxes and their lives as a whole. The act of letting go of what no longer nourishes us, of what weighs us down, demands both courage and discipline. This is why I often say that "the art of finding balance" is fundamentally "the art of letting go," even if it means releasing the persistent, self-inflicted nesting of guilt.

Ultimately, I encourage women to choose their battles with wisdom and intention. Sometimes, the truest victories lie in pursuing grander aspirations and conquering significant challenges, rather than being ensnared by the chattering "mind monkeys" of gossip, maid issues or closets.

To actively reclaim your time and energy and foster a greater sense of balance, consider these practical strategies:

1. **Focus Your Fire: The 80/20 Rule of Prioritisation.** Don't let your efforts be scattered. Apply the Pareto principle: identify the 20% of your tasks that deliver 80% of the results and concentrate your energy there.

Ruthlessly eliminate or delegate the less impactful activities to create more space.

2. **Find Your Center: The Anchor of Mindfulness.** In the midst of demanding schedules, cultivate regular mindfulness practices. These moments of quiet reflection can help restore your inner equilibrium, providing a much-needed respite from the external pressures that can so easily throw your feminine balance off-kilter.
3. **Lean on Your Network: Building Support Systems.** Don't hesitate to ask for help. Build a strong network of resources and actively seek support from your family, spouse, community, and workplace. Creating these support enablers allows you to share the load and avoid feeling overwhelmed.
4. **Schedule Self-Care: Your Essential "Me Time."** Protect your personal time fiercely. Block out specific slots in your calendar for self-care activities. Whether it's a simple indulgence like a pedicure, a revitalising workout, or cherished moments with loved ones, these dedicated times are non-negotiable investments in your well-being.

Build your own village

"Though the road may wind, and the burdens feel heavy, for the woman with an unyielding spirit:

Never let your vision dim, keep its fire burning bright.

Embrace your dreams, let them fuel your relentless drive.

Silence the voices of the shallow and the fleeting. Their opinions hold no sway.

Trust instead the unwavering voice that echoes within your own heart.

Build your own village, a circle of trust and support.
With courage as your armour, hope as your weapon, and honour as your shield,
Advance, dear sister, one deep breath at a time, one determined step at a time."

– Mishti Verma

Decluttering for Clarity and Balance: A Two-Jar Exercise

Feeling overwhelmed? This activity will help you identify what truly matters and consciously release what's holding you back. Grab two jars and some slips of paper.

Step 1: Defining Your Focus (The "I Choose to Focus On" Jar)

- Label one jar with the empowering statement: "I Choose to Focus On."
- Think about the tasks and priorities in your life that are truly critical – those with high importance and significant impact. Write each one down on a separate chit.
- As you place each chit into this jar, make a conscious commitment to dedicate your energy to these key areas until this jar represents your accomplished priorities.

Step 2: Releasing What No Longer Serves You (The "I Choose to Let Go Of" Jar)

- Label the second jar: "I Choose to Let Go Of."
- Now, reflect on what you need to release – perhaps it's a lingering obligation, a self-limiting belief, a time-wasting habit, or anything that feels like a burden. Write each of these on a separate chit.

- As you fill this jar, visualise yourself actively decluttering these items from your mental and emotional space. Your intention is to work towards emptying this jar, creating more lightness and freedom in your life.

CHAPTER 8

Seek-Beautiful Messy Strokes

Manic Monday Musings (aka My Brain on Overload):

Dear Me,

Okay, deep breaths. Today is officially one of *those* days. Work has decided to throw everything at me at once, the client is in full-on complaint mode, and my body is reminding me it has its own agenda (hello period cramps and a lovely new pimple). Plus, there's that important presentation hanging over my head, and the man I am dating has decided to contribute to the chaos with a perfectly timed disagreement – one I'm trying to smooth over while also keeping the client happy.

The thought of catching a flight tomorrow for another project feels almost surreal right now. In these moments of utter overwhelm, that little voice whispers, "Just be Wonder Woman!" But the reality is, I feel far from super. I feel like a hot mess express, and honestly, I'm just trying to survive.

And in these moments, the question arises: *Do I really need to be a Superhero?*

Superheroes soar through the sky with incredible powers, but the real strength of a "shero" lies not in capes and flight. Even with the constant demands pulling me in every direction, I don't need to be a superhero to navigate this. We don't need to achieve some flawless ideal and aim to become a masterpiece.

Instead, how about I see myself as an amazing abstract painting, constantly evolving, with different strokes for different folks. I am managing the beautiful chaos of the world in my own unique way, and finding happiness within that beautiful mess. I think this is being a superpower in itself.

Lots of love
Me

Survival Guide for Glorious Mess-Makers:

1. **Rock That Laundry Mountain:** Listen, sometimes the laundry pile reaches Everest proportions. And you know what? That's okay. Plant your glorious selfright in the middle of it, take a deep, dramatic breath, and just... exist. Feel the fabric. Contemplate the chaos. Then, when you're good and ready, tackle it one sassy sock at a time. This is a metaphor for life, so when there is a pile of problems staring at you, handle it one sassy problem at a time. You've got this, messy marvel!

2. **Unleash Your Inner Tiny Tornado:** Remember that little whirlwind of a girl who loved finger-painting outside the lines? She's still in there, probably plotting some sparkly mischief. Let her out! Embrace the glorious goofs, the happy accidents, the artistic explosions that might not make sense to anyone else. Giggle till your sides hurt, laugh like a hyena at a bad joke, and let your spontaneous inner child run wild. Messy fun is the best kind of fun!
3. **Bust a Move Like Your Hair's on Fire:** Want to twirl in the rain like a soggy noodle? Go for it! Feel the rhythm in your soul and dance like nobody's got their eyeballs glued to you (because honestly, they're probably too busy dealing with their own beautiful mess). Unleash your inner disco queen, your awkward ballet superstar – whatever in life moves you! Go for it full-throttle, unapologetically.
4. **Own That Stain Like a Boss:** Period leaks? Spilled coffee? Life happens, darling! Our bodies are amazing, and yes, sometimes they have a mind of their own. Menstrual flow is natural, powerful, and a badge of honour, and so are the little goof-ups in life that feel like stains. So, ditch the shame! Embrace the flow, the ebb and the... occasional oops. Remember that iconic tagline? Sometimes, *daag achche hain* (stains are good)! Own it, rock it, and keep being your magnificent, wonderfully real self.

Embracing Your Beautifully Imperfect Self: An Inner Child Journey

1. **Connecting with Your Inner Landscape:** Find a comfortable position and gently close your eyes. Take a few slow, deep breaths, allowing your body to soften.

Imagine turning your awareness inward, seeking that tender space within where your younger self resides – the little one who experienced the world with all its messy wonders and inevitable stumbles. Place a hand on the part of your body that feels connected to this inner child, a place of gentle holding and presence.

Whisper a question into that space: *What do you need right now to feel truly loved and seen?* Listen quietly for any sensations, images, or words that arise. Take a few more slow, deep breaths, and then offer these words to your inner child: *I hear you. You are whole and complete, exactly as you are, with all your beautiful mess and all your unique imperfections. I love you. I accept you fully. I forgive you for any perceived missteps and I ask for your forgiveness too.*

Journal your experiences.

2. **The Language of Touch and Colour: An Imperfect Masterpiece:** Now, gather some paints in colours that call to you, trusting your intuition. Using both hands, let your fingers become your brushes. On a blank surface (paper, canvas, anything you have), allow your hands to move freely, guided by instinct rather than intention. Explore different movements, create your own unique strokes. There is no right or wrong way to do this. Embrace the tactile sensation, the blending of colours, the delightful mess that might unfold. This is your expression, your imperfectly perfect creation.

Journal your experiences!

The secret of giggles!

You often ask me the secret of my giggles.
You often wonder what's so funny.
And then I wonder too. Why do I giggle like a young girl in school?
Why do I create ripples of laughter in a small pool?
Or clown around as if I were performing on stage.
Shouldn't I look all serious, formal and act my age!
Well, I really can't find profound answers to that, even with big glasses or in philosophy classes!
All I can find is a song in the wind.
All I can find are hidden moments like pearls hidden in shells.
All I can find is tranquil silence in the sound of divine bells.
All I can find is beauty in life and perceive life as magnificent art.
All I can find is a shrine of hope in the chambers of the heart.

– Mishti Verma

CHAPTER 9

Seeking Change

We've all heard the adage: "Nothing is permanent but change." Yet, the truth is, **embracing change is very difficult**. It's a concept we intellectually grasp but often emotionally resist. For women especially, change is an intrinsic part of our existence, mirroring the moon's phases. Our bodies transform, our lives unfold in distinct chapters, and we are constantly striving to cope, adapt, and evolve.

It's a continuous process, this dance with flux. And as I think about it, perhaps there's more to discover about this internal struggle. Perhaps it's time to explore these thoughts deeper through the pages of my journal, in notes to myself.

Note 1-The Fear of the Unknown: Running from Growth

Often, the mere thought of change fills us with such apprehension that we inadvertently **run away from the very growth that rests on its other side**. Change isn't just about external shifts; it demands new learning, which invariably requires us to step out of our comfort zones. It challenges us to take on new ventures, push past our perceived limitations, and confront those essential questions: "What's next? What am I restless about? What truly ignites my hunger?" If we aren't moving, growing, and seeking, we risk becoming like stagnant waters – still, uninspired, and ultimately, limited.

Note 2-The Illusion of Comfort: Stuckness vs. Stability

Consider the allure of a new job in a new city. Your gut instinctively knows it could be the next big leap, a pivotal moment. Yet, a part of you yearns to stay put, clinging to the familiar because it feels comforting. But beware: **on the other side of comfort often lies stuckness, stagnation, and profound limitation.**

We are conditioned to "settle down" – settling into a marriage, settling into a job. And yes, stability is wonderful; it provides a necessary period of rest and grounding. However, after that rest, we must awaken again to a new dawn, a fresh beginning, and a compelling call to action. True living isn't about perpetual rest; it's about continuous awakening.

Note 3-The Last Dance: A Story of Lost Calling

I once wrote a play called "The Last Dance," which explored this very struggle. It centered on Maria, a famous flamenco dancer whose passion for her art dwindled after a lost love and the onset of aging. Years later, by chance, she reconnects with Antonio, her former lover, who has also abandoned his artistic passion for painting and now leads a "regular," "settled" life. Both are long married, ostensibly content.

But within that comfort, there was a palpable void, a deep internal fracture. It wasn't the magic of lost love they yearned for; it was the **lost magic of their true calling**. At the end of their conversation, as a farewell, Antonio imparts a profound truth to Maria: "**Maria, do not kill yourself before you die**."

This searing statement jolts Maria into a stark realization. After 30 years of marriage, of living a "settled life," was that life truly making her feel alive? She had embraced many changes and phases of her life, yet she was still trapped in lost memories, paralyzed by the belief that she was too old to pursue her dreams.

Note 4-The Eagle's Rebirth: A Metaphor for Radical Transformation

There's a powerful story about the eagle that perfectly encapsulates the radical transformation required to truly embrace change. Eagles typically live between 20-30 years in the wild, though some can reach 70 years. To achieve this extraordinary lifespan, an eagle must make an incredibly difficult decision around its 40th year. At this age, its long, flexible talons can no longer effectively grasp prey. Its once-powerful beak becomes bent and dull, and its heavy, aged feathers cling to its chest, making flight arduous.

To undergo what is essentially a rebirth, the eagle retreats to a mountaintop. There, it painstakingly **plucks out its own talons, then repeatedly knocks its old beak against a rock**

until it breaks off. Once new talons and a new beak grow, it then **plucks out all of its old feathers**, one by one. This agonizing process takes months, but after this radical self-renewal, the eagle emerges, capable of another flight of life.

I've tried to capture the essence of this inspiring story in the poem that follows, a tribute to the courage required to embrace radical change.

An Eagle's Advice

I asked an Eagle,
"How could one fly like an eagle?
You have such powerful wings!"

The eagle looked from above and said,
"I pluck my own wings when they grow old
and restrict my flight.
It is a flight of change and pain,
a fight with myself for my flight,
till my new wings take shape again."

"Open your mind and see what is holding you back.
Let go; let the wind lift you up in the sky,
where there is more beyond the horizon.
The limitations rest in the mind;
the soul is always endowed with freedom!"

– Mishti Verma

Coaching Activity: Navigating Change Through Expressive Arts

Change can feel overwhelming, but expressive arts offer a powerful way to explore your feelings, identify roadblocks, and envision a path forward. This activity uses metaphor and visualization to help you gain clarity and momentum.

The Activity Steps

Here are the steps we can work through, either by drawing, journaling, or simply visualizing:

1. Metaphor of Current Change:

- What does the change you're facing *look* like? If this change were an object, a scene, or a symbol, what would it be? Take a moment to draw it, or simply describe it vividly in your mind and write your thoughts.

2. Inner Feelings & Connection:

- As you look at or imagine this metaphor of change, what **inner feelings** arise? What emotions are present in your body and mind?

3. The Path Forward:

- Considering this change, what do you believe **needs to happen** for you to move through it effectively? What are the essential next steps or shifts in perspective?

4. Identifying Roadblocks:

- What is **stopping you** from taking those steps or making those shifts? What are the internal or external **roadblocks** that stand in your way?

5. Transforming the Metaphor:

- How does your initial metaphor need to be **transformed** to better support you in embracing this change? Imagine it evolving into something that empowers you. If you drew it, make a new drawing. If you visualized it, spend time reshaping it in your mind.

6. Describing the New Vision:

- Write or speak a few lines that **describe this transformed metaphor**. What does it represent now? How does it feel different?

7. Support for Transformation:

- Now, looking at this new, transformed image or vision, what **support** do you need to fully embrace this transformation? This could be internal resources, external help, or new beliefs.

8. Small Action Step:

- What is one **small, tangible action** you can take today, or within the next 24 hours, towards embodying this transformation?

CHAPTER 10

Seeking the Small and Making it 'Big'

Social media often presents a glossy, idealized version of life, turning what should be inspiration into a relentless pursuit of aspiration. We scroll, we compare, and before we know it, we're caught in a subtle but potent trap of coveting our neighbour's "bigger car," "bigger house," "big fat wedding," and "bigger vacation." The mantra of "big is beautiful" echoes in our minds, fuelling a cycle of desire that's often more delusional than fulfilling. This relentless loop of aspiration ensnares us in ego traps of comparison and competition, leaving us constantly wanting more.

Last year, I felt a strong pull toward the mountains. Immediately, my mind began to conjure elaborate fantasies of a grand, luxurious getaway. Yet, as fate would have it, a series of commitments arose, leaving no room to unplug and embark on that dreamed-of escape.

In my despair, I sought to mend my own thought process. I began to reframe my perspective: why chase the "big" when the core desire was simply to be in the mountains? I realized I had several leadership training offsites already scheduled, all conveniently located closer to the hills. Instead of appreciating these smaller moments—where I was actively engaged in training in the hills—I was fixated on a fantasy of a "big luxury vacation in the hills."

And when the much awaited moment of the training event arrived, I was instantly enveloped in what felt like a big hug from the surrounding hills. A glorious sunrise brushed my forehead, a quiet acknowledgment, and I realized I couldn't quite articulate the sheer joy of resting in the lap of nature. But I know this feeling well: this is happiness.

Happiness isn't a distant dream, nor is it "somewhere over the rainbow." It resides in the power of the present moment. It's about what you create right now, in this very instant, that can stir an ocean of possibilities and new waves of joy.

Paradoxically, chasing the small can lead to truly monumental outcomes. Consider ants: individually tiny, but immense in number. Through consistent, small, everyday efforts, they gather food and collectively achieve significant transformations.

Similarly, small efforts pave the way for bigger wins. Small moments, when truly embraced, can lead to monumental leaps of faith and genuine celebrations of success.

Here are two small poems that express these sentiments:

> "As a little girl, whenever I drew mountains, I'd paint the sunrise nestled between them; maybe it's simply how we were shown. But as I grew and experienced life's own peaks and valleys, the magic of the mountains called me to discover my *own* sunrise."
>
> – Mishti Verma

> "I was always waiting for something "big" to unfold—a big surprise, a big opportunity, a big haul of dreams and goodies! And then one day, the sweetest moments came to me in small cups of life"
>
> – Mishti Verma

Coaching Activity: Unearthing Everyday Joy

This activity is designed to help you actively discover and appreciate the small moments of joy that often go unnoticed. By engaging with these practices, you'll cultivate a greater sense of presence and gratitude.

1. The Joy Cultivator Pot

Materials: A small pot, paints/markers/decorations that represent joy, a plant seed, soil, water.

Instructions:

- **Decorate your pot:** Take some time to personalize your small pot. Paint or draw elements, symbols, or colours that genuinely express joy to you. This isn't about artistic skill, but about infusing the pot with your personal essence of happiness.

- **Plant your seed:** Place a seed in the pot with soil.
- **Daily ritual:** Each day, as you water your plant, consciously repeat this affirmation aloud: "**The power of joy is in the here and now. I am happy and grateful for all that I have.**"
- **Reflection:** Observe the growth of your plant. How does this daily ritual connect you to the idea of nurturing joy in your own life? What parallels can you draw between the plant's growth and your own journey towards greater happiness?

2. The Joyful Moments Box

Materials: A small box, decorating supplies (optional), small slips of paper, a pen.

Instructions:

- **Prepare your box:** Decorate the small box in a way that feels joyful to you. This will be your "Joyful Moments Jar."
- **Identify small joys:** On individual slips of paper, write down **tiny moments that bring you happiness.** These are simple, often overlooked pleasures. Examples might include: "enjoying a cup of tea in silence," "calling a friend just to say hello," "listening to my favourite song without distraction," "watching the sunrise," or "taking a slow walk."
- **Conscious fulfillment:** Throughout your day or week, make a deliberate effort to **experience one of these moments**.
- **Acknowledge and release:** Once you've completed a joyful moment, **tear up the corresponding slip of paper**. This act symbolizes integrating that joy into your present experience and letting go of the need to hold onto the idea of it.

- **Reflection:** How does actively seeking out and experiencing these small moments shift your perspective on your day? What new small joys are you discovering?

3. Small Steps, Big Gains

Materials: A planner, notebook, or digital task list.

Instructions:

- **Identify a larger goal:** Choose one **bigger goal or desired outcome** you're working towards.
- **Break it down:** List **small, actionable tasks** that contribute to this larger goal. These tasks should be manageable and achievable in a relatively short amount of time. For example, if your bigger goal is "write a book," small tasks might be "write one paragraph," "outline a chapter," or "research a character."
- **Track your progress:** Write these small tasks in your planner or on your to-do list.
- **The power of the strike-off:** As you complete each small task, **strike it off your list**. Notice the satisfaction this simple act brings.
- **Reflection:** How does breaking down a large goal into small steps make it feel more attainable? How does tracking your progress motivate you?

4. Celebrate Every Victory

Instructions:

- **Conscious celebration:** Make it a point to **celebrate every small success**, no matter how minor it seems. This could be completing all your small tasks for the day, having a productive conversation, or even just sticking to your commitment to a joyful moment.

- **Methods of celebration:** Your celebration can be simple: a mental high-five, a quick happy dance, a grateful note in a journal, or sharing your success with a trusted friend.
- **Reflection:** How does celebrating small wins impact your overall motivation and sense of accomplishment? What shifts do you notice in your mindset when you intentionally acknowledge your progress?

By consistently engaging with these activities, you'll train your mind to seek out and appreciate the profound impact of small moments, cultivating a deeper, more sustainable sense of joy in your life.

CHAPTER 11

Hide and Seek of Resilience

The new year had just begun. While some revelled in the afterglow of celebrations, my day unfolded differently. I was with a senior leader, offering a space of hope as the leader navigated difficult challenges. It struck me then that the new year doesn't hold the same story for everyone.

For some, the quiet victory lies in their strength to keep going. In that moment, a poem for the new year began to stir within me, one that honoured not just joy, but also the quiet celebrations of resilience.

Your own earth

"If you are looking for some sunshine
and find darkness all around
Through the cracks and crevices,
through a little window of hope
Let light come in!
If you want to feel the wind in your hair
And all doors are shut
Uncage your soul, breathe freely, breathe deeply!
If you want to feel the soil beneath your feet
And all you have sight of, are faraway lands

Whatever it takes and whatever it's worth, my friend,
find your own earth!"

– Mishti Verma

To access our inner world of resilience, psychodrama utilizes group dynamics and dramatic devices, revealing fascinating concepts such as 'Tele' and 'sociometry.'

Imagine it as the unseen threads of feeling that draw us closer to some people and create a distance with others in a group.

'Tele' speaks to how we unconsciously develop connections with those around us. It unfolds a natural affinity for some and a subtle separation from others.

In the safe space of a psychodrama group, 'Tele' becomes important. As people explore their emotions through acting out their experiences, they begin to understand these unseen connections. This process can deepen their awareness of their feelings and how they relate to others, ultimately fostering resilience, a powerful sense of belonging and shared strength.

It was a gift to witness the warmth of human connection while working with a community of coaches for a radio show on applied executive coaching in South Africa. There, I felt the deep meaning of 'ubuntu' – an ancient African word that speaks of our shared humanity. It wasn't just in the greetings exchanged, but in the subtle, compassionate ways people interacted; a beautiful and invisible web of kindness.

I've often tried to cultivate this same feeling in my workshops. By allowing time for a sense of 'tele' – that unspoken understanding – and group connection to grow, I've seen how people naturally connect. Through simple things like shared breaths, gentle eye contact, and open greetings, a supportive tapestry begins to weave itself as bodies move and find their distinct ways to connect.

It's natural to be drawn to those who offer a safe harbour to reach out to.

These individuals are our lighthouses, unwavering cheerleaders, and steadfast support buddies. When life's currents push us into challenging waters, it's a comfort to know we have resources – our own ability to troubleshoot and our supportive "resilience mascots".

That inner resilience I felt often resembled a warrior's resolve. Life's path, full of its own surprises, led me to an uncanny connection with it. While shaping a resilient character, I crossed paths with military veterans. Little did I know then that they would have such a strong influence in my life, and I learned some of the greatest lessons during my interactions with them. But the strongest lesson was that integrity is not a choice, it is character; resilience is not a choice, it is a matter of discipline. It was in building those bridges that I unexpectedly discovered deeper wells of inner strength, a quiet resilience I didn't know I possessed, and a never-give-up attitude.

Through my connection with another inspiring "resilience mascot," I began to truly understand the beautiful magic of 'tele' – that unspoken understanding between people.

I was particularly touched by the story of our country's first visually impaired aerobic trainer. She faced many obstacles, yet blossomed into a highly accomplished entrepreneur and author. From her, I learned about the incredible power of our other senses, how they can open up a world of connection far beyond what we might perceive through sight alone and the indomitable spirit of the relentless seeker. Her story showed me that our ways of experiencing and connecting with the world are truly limitless.

I was so moved by her journey that I captured it in a theatre act, which was then brought to life by the legendary theatre actor Tom Alter and other actors from my team.

Here is an excerpt from the theatre piece, a resilient voice against stereotypes.

Application

(Woman sits on the stage under a single spotlight, directly addressing the audience with a warm, open gaze.)

Woman: I'm here today because I want to apply for a job. I am intelligent, well-educated, and very determined. And yes, I am a blind woman.

Voice: (A kind, slightly hesitant male voice from the shadows behind the stage) What are your qualifications?

Woman: I had the privilege of studying at one of the finest convent schools in New Delhi, right up until the eighth grade. After that, they suggested I leave, believing a school specifically for the blind would be more suitable.

Voice: Well, if you have musical abilities, perhaps you could apply for a position as a music teacher?

Woman: (A gentle smile touches her lips as she turns slightly towards the audience) A teacher, they said. For most women, that's just 'teacher.' But for a blind woman, it seems it must be 'music teacher.' And yes, I did teach music for a while.

But my world isn't just darkness. My other senses are vibrant, alive.

Voice: Then... then perhaps the most suitable role for you would be that of a housewife. You could certainly apply there!

Woman: (A soft sigh escapes her) I did. And it wasn't easy to get that job either. It seemed many men were interested in a girlfriend, not a wife. But I did get married. And while I held that particular 'job,' as you put it, my husband decided to leave his. He felt there was no need for him to work. He moved into my home, taking advantage of me and all the benefits until I decided to resign from the role of his wife.

Voice: (A note of finality in his tone) I'm afraid... I'm afraid there's nothing left for you then. Where would you find another husband? Perhaps... perhaps the only thing left is to simply give up.

Woman: (Her voice rises with a quiet but firm strength, and she slowly stands) NO. My world will not fade to black. (She pauses, then gently sits back down, a thoughtful expression on her face. After a moment, speaking softly but directly to the unseen voice) I... I have an idea.

Voice: (A flicker of curiosity in his tone) What is it? What idea?

Woman: Have you ever seen the Jane Fonda Aerobics videos?

Voice: (A pause, a hint of confusion) What? No, I haven't.

Woman: (A playful smile returns) From the sound of your voice... she seems to be from your generation. What a shame. Perhaps *you* should just give up.

Voice: (A touch of offence) Excuse me?

Woman: (Chuckles softly) Alright, alright. Let me try something more recent. The modern media influencers?... Their fitness DVDs?

Voice: Yes... so?

Woman: So... I am going to become an aerobics instructor.

Voice: (A burst of incredulous laughter) What?! You... you want me to say, 'Great idea!'? Okay, okay... now I think *I'm* going to die laughing! Ha ha ha...

Woman: (A gentle determination in her voice) Well, you will see. I'm leaving now.

Voice: (A hint of lingering scepticism) Why did you even come here in the first place? To ask for help?

Woman: (A serene smile) No. To find the answers.

(Woman slowly exits the stage. The spotlight remains, and the light subtly shifts.)

(After a moment, the Woman re-enters, now wearing a different accessory – perhaps a scarf or a piece of jewellery. She walks with a newfound confidence and sits down at a table, as if in a coffee shop, nearly bumping into the unseen Voice.)

Voice: (A surprised tone) Oh, look who it is. After all these years. I never thought we'd meet again. What answers are you searching for now?

Woman: (A warm smile) Just came for a cup of coffee. Is that a problem?

Voice: No, no. But... I do have a question.

Woman: (A knowing look) And the answer is... God helps those who help themselves. And if you ask, you will receive.

Voice: So… did you get the job?

Woman: (A quiet pride in her voice) Yes. And I built a career. I'm sure you're curious to know how. I went to a very popular aerobics instructor and asked her to teach me. I waited in her office for three hours, refusing to leave until she agreed. So, I asked for her help and kept asking until I received it. My classes became popular. I would run two or three sessions a day. People saw results, and they were happy. I have applied for and been successful in several roles since then – from being a marketing head of a company to a corporate trainer, and now… a successful entrepreneur and author.

Voice: (A genuine sound of applause from the background) I… I never thought you would achieve such great things. You truly deserve applause. Wonderful. So, I suppose you don't need a husband now. You are an independent, strong woman.

Woman: (A soft smile) Well, I did want to get married again. And I was very determined about that, too.

Voice: Then… I think I can assume you did.

Woman: (A gentle nod) Yes, I did. Against all odds. I married someone ten years younger than me.

Voice: (A warm smile in his voice) Does this sound like a happy ending?

Woman: (A thoughtful pause) It's not the end. It's just a little pause. A moment to step out… until we meet again.

Voice: How will you… How will you manage? Will you need a cane to cross?

Woman: (A serene smile) I don't need a cane. I never learned Braille, and I don't need a cane. I will simply ask for help from someone in this lovely audience. Many times, I travelled by public transport to my office in Delhi. Sometimes, someone was assigned to help me cross the road, as the office was just opposite the bus stop. But they would often be late. So, I would simply get off the bus and ask someone, "Bhaiya ji, please help me cross the road?" And before you ask... no, no one ever tried to take advantage. And yes, I am talking about Delhi. They simply helped. I believed in human canes, in building bridges of trust. So, I will just ask some wonderful person here to guide me to the door.

- **Reflection:** Who are the individuals in your social circles who inspire your strength and offer reliable support? List two to three people.
- **Mapping:** Draw a quick map of your social network. Highlight those you consider your "resilience mascots."

Construct Your Bridge of Connection:

- **Identification:** If you were building a bridge of support, which three to five people would be your key pillars? What specific support could each offer?
- **Action Planning:** Choose one person from your identified pillars. What small step can you take this week to strengthen that connection?

Discover Your Inner Strength:

- **Introspection:** What are the two to three core strengths or past experiences that have helped you overcome challenges?
- **Affirmation:** Write down two to three "I am..." statements that reflect your inner resilience (e.g., "I am resourceful," "I am determined").

CHAPTER 12

Hide and Seek of Love

You know that feeling? The harder you chase after love, the more it plays hide-and-seek. It's like it's got a radar for desperation. But the moment you stop looking, when you're just living your life, BAM! Love shows up in the most unexpected ways. It's a weird, beautiful dance, isn't it?

Real stories have been hidden, and fairytales have been sold to us in novels and movies. We're sold this dream of a perfect romance, a love that fills every empty space and void.

We have yearned for the canvas of 'navras' of 'shringar,' the play of 'ras leela' and the whole enchanting 'maya' of love. And when we're thirsty for that connection of true love, we wander through our internal deserts, searching for an oasis that keeps disappearing. Turns out, it's just a mirage.

I see it all the time in my work: incredible women, brilliant and strong, but carrying this weight of 'not enough.' We're constantly asking ourselves, 'Am I pretty? Am I lovable?' Think of that haunting question: 'Mirror, mirror, on the wall, who's the fairest of them all?' It's a question we've all asked, in some way or another, thanks to the relentless pressure to conform to impossible beauty standards. In Snow White, that magic mirror became the queen's obsession, a tool to measure her worth against an ever-shifting idea. The mirror's honesty, ironically, became her undoing because it revealed the futility of chasing an illusion. Our worth isn't a competition; it's a truth we hold within ourselves.

Think about it: even today, 'fair' skin is still a selling point in marriage ads. We're still trapped in this outdated beauty standard. The need is to be 'fair' in embracing equitable beauty standards and not get swept by 'fair and lovely' mindsets.

We're sold this lie that something's missing, that we need someone else to complete us. This 'lack' creates a hunger, a desperate need for validation. And so, we search in all the wrong places, get our hearts broken, and end up hiding in shame, afraid to face the world. And the drama of 'hide and seek' continues.

Women, through a romantic lens, are often seen as the Moon. Well, if we are the moon, this could be our soul verse:

Moon

And the moon says,
Don't look at me with belonging, I belong to another sky
Tomorrow, you may search for me in vain
And find just a glimpse of a half-moon, through the window pane
Still in glory, with no shame

I will shine,
As the incomplete is as beautiful as your imperfections
And the scars are as beautiful as the stars
Don't look at me,
Lost lovers in search of the promise of love
Love is not found in the moon, stars and sweet nothings
It is found in the purity of the heart and the eyes of naked truth
Or on the paths of wilderness, paths of faith and surrender
Beyond the meeting and parting of ways, there lies a union
When the incomplete finds completion
And then a day comes
When you find the full moon, shining unabashedly in the arms of the sky

– Mishti Verma

Like the beautiful moon, we're a whole cycle, a whole journey. We've got our bright days and our dark nights, our full moons and our slivers. And when we finally look in the mirror and say, 'Yeah, this is me, all of it,' that's when the magic happens. That's when we stop hiding, stop apologising for being human. That's when we step into our wholeness, and guess what? Love—real, unabashed love—finds us. Because what we have been looking for... It's been looking for us, too.

And when love arrives, we stumble into old patterns, don't we? We start the endless questioning: 'Is this it? Is this the one?' We chase commitment, security, marriage, that external validation, while simultaneously hiding pieces of ourselves, afraid of rejection. But here's the truth: our partners aren't saviours, they're mirrors. They reflect what's already within us. They don't complete us; we complete ourselves. The real marriage, the lasting union, happens within. It's about embracing the 'Shiva' and 'Shakti,' the 'Yin' and 'Yang' within, finding our purpose, the path that ignites our soul. When that inner ceremony is complete, life sends its signals, those quiet signposts pointing us towards a partner ready for a true, purpose-driven partnership.

Badhu Bela

Dressed for marriage,

She adorned herself with flowers and jewellery.

Admiring how she looked in the mirror

She completed the last strokes of Shringar

A Big Red Bindi and laced her eyes with kajal

A smile of contentment, inner whispers telling her

That she looked beautiful and divine!

She was ready to leave for the altar, and then a slight nervous thought – "Let me look at myself one last time, just one final look, the hope for perfection!"

And this time, when she looked into the mirror, suddenly something changed....

She saw a reflection of her beloved instead

Surprised, she looked again

And again, a reflection of her beloved!

Had he become the mirror, or she the reflection

She wondered..

Or had she become the reflection, and he the mirror

She wondered...

Maybe she was wearing his favourite colour of saree

So his memory transformed into a reflection

But then she realised, it was not a memory, it was something perhaps beyond the chains of the mind.
In this golden light, also known as 'Badhu Bela,' the moment of golden dusk, where the bride shines in radiant beauty.
In this golden light of grace, she was seeing him in her, and her in him
Maybe it was not about mirrored reflections anymore
Maybe the reflection and mirror had become one
The lover and the beloved had become one
Maybe the bride dropped her 'veil'
The Shiva and the Shakti had become one
Maybe the marriage had already happened!

– Mishti Verma

Activity: Heart of Self-Love

This activity is designed to help you connect with your inner self, cultivate self-love, and celebrate your wholeness.

Materials:

- Paper or canvas
- Paints, markers, crayons, or coloured pencils
- Glitter, sequins, fabric scraps, or other decorative materials
- Mirror

Instructions:

1. **Create Your Heart:**
    - On your paper or canvas, draw a heart. This heart represents your heart – the center of your being.
    - Take your time and allow the shape to feel right to you. There's no "perfect" heart.

2. **Decorate with Intention:**
    - Decorate your heart with the materials you've chosen. As you add each element, consider what it represents about you.
        - What colours resonate with your emotions?
        - What textures feel comforting or joyful?
        - Do the decorations symbolise your strengths, passions, or dreams?
    - Imagine rays of light emanating from your heart, symbolising your inner radiance and the love you have to offer the world.
3. **Words of Your Heart:**
    - Around your heart, write a few words or short phrases that describe the essence of your art. These could be words that:
        - Capture how you feel while creating it.
        - Express your unique qualities.
        - Remind you of your worth.
4. **Affirm Your Wholeness (21-Day Practice):**
    - Stand in front of a mirror.
    - Look into your eyes and say the following affirmations with conviction and self-compassion:
        - "I love and accept myself totally and fully."
        - "I am whole, I am complete."
    - Repeat these affirmations daily for 21 days. This consistent practice helps to integrate these truths into your subconscious and cultivate a deeper sense of self-love.
5. **Dance to Your Heart's Rhythm:**
    - Place both hands gently on your heart.
    - Close your eyes and tune in to the rhythm of your heartbeat.
    - Allow your body to move intuitively, following your natural rhythm.

- You may find yourself swaying, stepping, or moving in ways that feel unique and expressive.
- Hum a tune, a melody that arises from your heart. This could be a simple, repetitive sound or a more complex melody. There is no right or wrong way to do this.
- This movement and sound are an expression of your heart's song – a celebration of your unique life force.

CHAPTER 13

Seeking Shakti

In the grip of darkness, the human spirit yearns for illumination. And when touched by empowerment, we instinctively seek 'shakti'—the feminine essence that flows through everything, the very source of creation's dance.

The creation's dance bestowed upon me the final challenge—a storm before clear skies could emerge. The contrast was stark: the judge called us for the divorce hearing while my ex-husband was preoccupied, casually chatting with his new girlfriend. Stepping out of the thorn-filled shoes of a wife, I was forced to immediately adopt the role of a responsible parent to a man acting like an irresponsible teenager, completely oblivious to the gravity of the moment. We finally signed the document with no goodbyes exchanged. As I left, he had someone waiting for him at the door. I had no one waiting for me, but I saw an image of myself at the door, a woman mounting a horse; some battles had been won. With the end of one institution, another of true liberation had to be written.

As life went by, I subsequently underwent a significant shift.

The buoyancy that once propelled me faded, and I retreated inward. The spring in my step vanished, replaced by a deep inclination to hide. Those who had witnessed my former vitality would often remark, with a knowing smile, that I had built a solitary tower around myself. And like Rapunzel, only my long hair—my carefully guarded self—might cascade through a window, and only when I consciously chose to let it down. The solitary path I walked unexpectedly led me into a profound exploration of spirituality, a crucible for forging resilience. My faith deepened in the quietude of that inner journey, a willing surrender unfolding within. And on those mystical, internal trails, I was gifted glimpses of a golden, healing light, a tangible sense of the *devi* woven into the fabric of everyday existence, appearing in countless subtle and extraordinary ways.

I remember painting a simple pot at my cultural centre when my brushes, guided by an unseen hand, spontaneously revealed the form of the *devi* – with wide, knowing eyes, a prominent *bindi*, and an extended tongue. Later, when I launched the gender sensitisation forum, a voice rising against ingrained stereotypes, that very image of the *devi* mystically found its place at the heart of the campaign. Even before consciously directing my prayers to her, I was being led, drawn to her presence.

Even as I worked with thousands of women across countless platforms, empowering them to discover their own 'inner shakti,' I later recognized that her footprints had always been present, guiding my path.

Initially, I hadn't grasped that this was my path of 'purpose,' and that the path of purpose is inherently one of empowerment.

We were, in essence, writing our destinies with the vibrant red ink of empowerment, acknowledging the inner goddess residing within us all. This awakening of the feminine principle, perhaps transcending the very constructs of gender, lying behind the masculine and the feminine, is an expression of *prakriti* – our fundamental power to create and recreate from the very womb of purpose and empathy, navigating chaos and emotions with a fierce declaration of freedom.

Yet, the echoes of fear persisted in so many of my workshops. It was time for a resurgence of voices, a breaking free from the suppression of the feminine lineage, confined to the dusty pages of history and the hushed corners of our hearts.

And so, I began *Inner Katha*, not as the end of a story, resting just at one destination, but as a caravan for self-expression, a journey for all genders to embrace their *shakti*, to reclaim their voices, and to seek their authentic identities by shedding societal masks.

For as we seek the paths of the divine, or our own unique representation of the higher forces of the universe, we are guided towards deeper stories and uncharted paths within. And in this seeking, a tender, sweet girl who weathered life's storms and built anew – navigating divorce, the quiet sorrow of unrealised motherhood, the birth of a pioneering cultural centre, and the purposeful expansion of business – now sees her story as a story of metamorphosis, beckoning her to become a warrior of light.

Holding the hand of this warrior of light, I bow to the light in you, and pose the pivotal question: Empowerment – is it found in the hiding, in the refuge of our shadows, or in the seeking of our naked truth? The real question we must ask ourselves...

Prakriti – Ode to the feminine

They called her a witch,
Burnt for knowing nature's secrets and beyond.
They sought to hide her behind a veil,
They sought to hide her power.
She is abused and violated,
They tie her to social chains,
They have chained her from times and beyond.
But she knows the secrets of nature and beyond.
She is Prakriti, nature, feminine, and beyond.
She cannot be controlled,
Her power is beyond.
She not only gives birth but creates eternally.
She is Prakriti!
Don't try to steal her secrets,
They are to be discovered.
Harm nature, and disasters unfold from times and beyond.
Sit under her shade, you will feel protected and sheltered.
You feel the wind caress you and lull you to sleep.
She will empower you and free you from your own chains.
She is freedom, Prakriti, the feminine, and beyond!

– Mishti Verma

CHAPTER 14

Soul Whispers

The empowered voices of women from our workshops, without their professional labels – just soul whispers.

"This helped me to find my inner self. I made a change in my life to move from a male-dominated role to a female-oriented family management. This session helped me focus on financial wellness as a result of the change I made."

Kavita

It helped me trace that "fun-loving and active me" who was lost in the busy schedules and pressure, and now I vow I will not let her go. I will stay focused. After the activities, I feel very light and ready to accept the abundant energy and all that is there for me.

Naznin

Helped me remove that fear in me that I never thought was there. I will introspect, and only then will the transcending happen.

Zarine

I always felt I had good control of everything. But suddenly, when the situation changed, I started feeling guilty. But after this session, I feel it is OK. Concentrating on myself is more important. I realised that innate balance in me. Though, at present, due to the situation, there is a little imbalance, I am confident that I can restore it. Thanks for this great session.

Myrtle

I love to be a superwoman, and to be this, I try to be happy and make everyone around me happy; I make a genuine effort. But, I realised that in doing all this, I feel I have never connected with myself and have not focused on what I want to do in life..

Hansika

Global Whispers:

Gendered voices from global coaches and expressive arts therapists.

"When gender challenges intersect with other aspects of identity, they compound to make the situation worse. I also believe that people often live in their own identity silo and have no empathy or understanding for any other "silo". In contrast, we could do more together. There is power in intersectionality. Stop, feeling the need to shrink or to be the balloon that deflates to not take up space and to be less visible."

Colleen Qvist
COMENSA MASTER COACH (CMC)
COMENSA MASTER MENTOR (CMM)

A Conversation of Two Selves

Who are you?
I mean really, who are you?
Who am I?
I am that which you are becoming.
I am a whole and total universe.
I am often hidden, even derided/ misunderstood.
I am often not heard, or I am often misheard.
Oh.
I have a whole world inside!
A wholeness of difference
Lurking in the Shadowy spaces
I wear a Mask for you to see me.
Changing so others can see you see me.
Sometimes the mask fits, and other times not.
Sometimes wearing the Mask feels like a round peg fitting in a square hole.

Seen and Not seen.
Pegged or Not Pegged
A 'Not as.......'(fill in the blank.)
-Rise above it!
Beyond these barriers (they are always there)
Practice. I am one
Who will speak to those ready and willing to listen
Who embraces the Both/Within the infinite of the circle.
All that exist
For a way forward
From the Shadows
of the voiceless
to the Voiceful.

– Jennie Kristel, MA, REAT, RMT APTT
Journey Works LLC
Registered Expressive Arts Therapist

Oneness Through Verse

One colour

I am not just black or white,
not pink or blue.
No labels of gender or culture define me.
I'm not bound by a social verdict of good or bad.

I am the colours of a carnival,
colours of life's celebration.
I am the colours of the warm sun,
colours of strength and hope.
I am the colours of the flag, celebrating a republic's freedom.
I am the colours of the green earth,
colours of nurturing and belonging.

I am the colour of light,
where the world isn't divided by colour,
where all colours dissolve into one light,
in peace, in oneness!

– Mishti Verma

Masterpiece

Where lies the beauty?
With the artist, or in the art?
Where lies the power?
With the creator, or in the creation?
Where lies the magic?
With lovers, or in their love?

A wise sage tells me, it's in neither.
The answers unfold as the veil drops,
and the soul bares itself in wonder.
Dropping the robes of ego, fear, and separation,
in that moment of union of art and artist,
of creation and creator,
of love and the lovers—
in that moment of oneness—
lies 'om'nipotence and liberation
There lies the masterpiece!

– Mishti Verma

Suggested Reading on Themes Explored in the Book

On Expressive Arts and Psychodrama:

Free Play: Improvisation in Life and Art
by Stephen Nachmanovitch

The Creative Connection: Expressive Arts as Healing
by Natalie Rogers

The Living Stage: A Step-by-Step Guide to Psychodrama, Sociometry and Experiential Group Therapy
by Tian Dayton

On Proxemics:

The Hidden Dimension
by Edward T. Hall

On Friedrich Nietzsche:

Beyond Good And Evil
by Friedrich Nietzsche